GW01459085

This book
is dedicated
to all
Christs

The God Book

By

Prem Raja Baba

Formerly titled
Being A God On The Planet Earth

ISBN 0-9645010-3-1

Published by

Prem Raja Baba
Post Office Box 1401
Mount Shasta, California 96067

ANALOGIES OF BEING A GOD

Humans are like icebergs (or maybe icebergs are like humans). We only see a small portion of an iceberg, the major part hidden under the ocean surface. That is the part that is powerful enough to have taken many ships to the bottom. Even though it is not seen, it does not mean that it is not there, nor that it is not part of the iceberg. It, like our God-self, is very much part of the iceberg and is just as real as the rest of us.

Imagine you are given a car and have never driven one or been trained in the proper operation of a car. You are told how to start it, put it in forward and reverse gear and use the brakes. No one has told you about the accelerator pedal, so you creep around town at idle thinking that this is as fast as it goes. It is only when someone who knows how to tap into the real power of your car and shows you how to do that, do you discover your car's true power and really start to enjoy driving.

The God Book is just like that. Most humans have been creeping around at idle, not knowing about just how powerful they are or how to tap into that power. This book tells you about your power and shows you how to tap into it and exercise it every moment of your day.

REALITY AND BELIEFS

There is a difference between reality and belief. Belief is what a person holds to be true in the absence of proof. When a person finds a particular belief important, they sometimes search for bits of proof to substantiate their belief. Some of these bits are like when a person prays to God for something and they receive it. To them, this is proof that there is a God.

There is a God. The only difference between what most people now believe as true and what is shown in this book is that they believe that there is one God for everyone and everything in the universe. This book shows and proves how each of us is an individual God.

When you combine the truth that is in this book with the experience of receiving something after praying for it, the only difference is that you realize that it has been you, as a God, that has answered your prayers all these years and not some God that you were taught to believe in.

Once you realize, through the work in this book, that you are a God, and that you can affect changes in your life effortlessly, that will be your irrefutable proof that you are a God, and no one else is in command of your life.

INTRODUCTION

Over the centuries, the majority has held many beliefs that have been since proven to be false. As late as 1492, many believed that the world was flat. Others believed that the Planet Earth was the center of the Universe and the Sun and stars all revolved around it. Even as I progressed on my spiritual path, new knowledge and experiences made old truths obsolete, null and void.

For years, I was on a path of Ascension. I was taught that Ascension was what a soul did to become an Ascended Master. What an Ascended Master was, I was not sure. Jesus was an Ascended Master. So, once I had Ascended, I should be able to walk on water, heal people, and everything religion said he could do.

In 1990, I was told that I was an Ascended Master. My spirit guides told me and then I met a woman on Mt. Shasta, in Panther Meadows, a sacred place, who shared an experience she had. In this experience, she was in meditation and asked to be shown an Ascended Master. It was then that Babaji told her that I was an Ascended Master. I didn't feel or look any different and I sure couldn't walk on water. I had created a few miracles in my time, but not ones that Jesus did. I had to believe it since I received the information from two sources, both unsolicited.

Before I could accept that I was an Ascended Master I first had to have a belief that I could be an Ascended Master. As I continued to progress with my spiritual experiences, I began to be told that I was a God. At first, it was difficult to believe, since I didn't have any beliefs to support it and I had no hard evidence to confirm it. Still, I continued and slowly I discovered my powers and abilities.

I began creating my life on a daily basis. I created new healing modalities. I began to use commands that not only affected my own life, but seemed to have an effect on people all around the globe. My perception of life changed as my experiences changed and soon I realized and accepted that I truly was a God. Once I realized that I was a God, I soon realized that so was everyone else. I could see it even if they could not.

From there, it took years of making commands before I discovered that I could also make laws. All the rituals and meditations and other spiritual games I had played were obsolete. I felt sad since they were fun for me, but, in order for me to be a God, I had to exercise my powers and not go backwards, not even for the fun of it. Now my life was controlled by me through commands and laws.

I introduced commands in my first book, The Joy Book. There I told my readers that we were all Ascended Masters. I am not sure many of my readers could accept that and I am not so sure that you will be able to accept the fact that you are a God. I created the laws in the Personal Laws document in this book and feel sure that once you experience the changes in your life that will take place after signing these laws, it will convince you that you are truly a God.

I invite you to challenge your past truths of who you were told you are and embrace this book and allow it to take you to your real truth, that you are a God.

BEING A GOD

For some, God is a patriarchal white bearded old man in the sky, looking down on all of us like children having to be watched, cared for, rewarded and/or punished. For others, it is gods and goddesses like those in Greek mythology. Then again, some see "God" as Jesus or Jesus as "God". For a growing minority, "God" is seen as each individual human or to put it another way, each human being is experienced as an individual God.

Some Christians see all humans as gods with a little "g" and one God with a capital "G" that takes care of the universe. My experience is that while there is a God or Gods that rule and are responsible for major realms like planets, star systems, galaxies and the whole Universe, their prime focus is not to be responsible for humans. That is our own responsibility.

When people pray to God, they are actually praying to their own God Self. When their prayers are answered, it is actually their own God Self that took action, not the great God in the sky. When their prayers are not answered, it is usually due to personal laws in effect in our lives that prevents it.

We are all Gods with a capital "G". We are not sheep or children to be taken care of, judged, rewarded and/or punished. We have been kept in the dark, in fear and in ignorance of the truth for too long. It is time for us to retake our power. It is time for us to retake command of our lives and be the Gods that we are.

At this time in history, being a God on this planet is a real challenge. For one, it is not accepted as a reality, nor is it generally accepted as a belief. Talking about being a God to most people causes their discomfort level to rise. We are few and far between. It can get lonely at times unless we connect with others of our kind (Gods). Remember that the only difference between us and the rest of the world is that we are Gods and we know it, they are Gods, but don't know it.

Life wasn't always like this on Planet Earth. Ignorance really is bliss, for once we realize the truth of who we are, we can't go back. We have had better experiences on this planet, but at this time the planet is going through a major transition and these experiences have to temporarily be put on a back burner.

The transition we are attempting to effect is to totally liberate this planet from the pain, suffering, lack, ignorance, fear and darkness that has plagued humanity for thousands of years. To do this, we have had to sacrifice some of our God powers and even some creature comforts. This explains why so many people have asked why their lives are such a struggle at this time. We all have done enormous spiritual purifications and things never seem to change much. The reason for this is because whatever gains we achieve, we put them into the mission and not the improvement of our spiritual status on this planet.

My experiences have been that in order to change this planet, we must effect changes throughout the whole Universe. I am not sure whether this planet is a reflection of what is going on in the Universe or the Universe is a reflection of what is going on here or maybe both. What I do know is that this planet is the Jerusalem of the Universe, the spiritual center, where the royal palace and the kings, queens, emperors and empresses reside. This is where the Universe is ruled. I am not sure why, but it seems that in order for a God to rule, change or effect any part or the whole of the Universe, that

God must reside on this planet in a third dimensional body. That is why we reside on this planet in human bodies.

As Gods, we find this mission more important than any other experience on this planet. Our total focus is on the mission and only a bare minimum of our energy, priority and focus is placed on our human existence. Our human body is an aspect of our total God being. It is independent in many ways and unified in others. Unless we communicate with our God aspect and spell out our requirements, we will always get the bare minimum necessary to sustain life. We do this by making or enacting laws and making commands.

Laws are a structure that keeps our systems operating efficiently, reliably and by the specifications that we designated. Commands are what we use to create what we want in the moment. At times we use laws and commands in combination to create what we want.

When we were born on to this planet, we took on a set of personal laws that were a combination of our parents' laws and the laws that are in mass consciousness. This brought to us many laws that were guilt based, religion based, fear based, and ignorance based. I have worked for years to discover ways to repeal these laws and in essence, change the lives of all humanity. In the beginning, I used commands. I would make these commands every day. Sometimes, I would say these commands a few times a day. Sometimes that was not enough. The commands were effective in changing my life experiences, but were never permanent. It was only when I printed out all my commands on paper and signed them did I experience some permanence of the commands.

From there, I designed a document consisting of hundreds of laws to apply to my personal and Universal requirements. It worked well for me. I was reluctant to share my laws with others since they were so different from what people were used to experiencing spiritually. My friend, at that time, was having medical and physical problems that kept her disabled most of the time. Even sitting at her computer and writing was impossible for her. I took the basic laws from my laws and published a generic set of laws that would apply to her and anyone else. I printed a set of them out for her and had her sign them. In less than twenty four hours, she was up and about and had enormous energy. She sat down at her computer and wrote over one hundred laws in one day and added them to the set I had given her. From that time, her life improved daily. The pain from her fibromyalga lessened to a point where she rarely had to use any pain killers. She maintained a garden that summer, something she previously was unable to do.

After seeing the great effects the laws had on her, I shared them with other close friends, all with great success. Spirit guided many people to me that summer to sample them and give me feedback. I Emailed them to all the spiritual teachers and healers I knew and they began sharing them with their students and clients. After hearing many success stories, I decided that these laws must get out to the world. They are so advanced, I was unsure whether people were ready for them or not. At first, many were turned off by the highly technical wording of the laws, but as time went by more people were receptive to them. I wrote a mellow version of the laws, but found that most people were wanting the original version.

My spiritual guidance told me that I could sign the laws for anyone who I do healings on. So, I signed sets of laws on the behalf of all my students and all my clients. People who were experiencing problems would call me on the telephone and I would tell them about the laws. They would ask me to send a copy to them so they could sign the laws for themselves.

They would give me permission to sign a set on their behalf. Many felt immediate effects the moment I signed them.

One spiritual healer in Australia after signing the laws for her clients and giving them Command Subconscious Programs (see my book, The Joy Book) found them experiencing miracles.

A friend's lover had problems staying focused and conscious. When he signed the laws, he immediately began experiencing energy surges moving through his body. This went on for quite awhile as if there were hundreds of beings in his body that were bailing out. When the surges stopped, we all noticed that he was much more present and had no problems staying awake.

Another friend, after signing the personal laws, experienced an immediate increase in joy, her relationships improved and her business and income increased considerably. Her workload actually increased to the point where she had to hire someone to help her.

A friend that had been living in her RV for years, was severely environmentally sensitive and had been in an abusive relationship. She experienced major improvements in her life upon signing the laws. She was finally able to leave that abusive relationship. Her health improved and her energy level increased to the point where she was finally able to do her creative art work again. She was also able to move out of her RV and into a house.

For a long time I believed that thought was creative and that was all. I never believed in evil beings and for most of my life dismissed them as creations of religions to keep people in fear. As my spiritual awareness increased over the years, I realized that there are what can be called evil beings, or evil gods. I define them as any beings that imposes its will on another and/or is conditional. This is opposite to what I define as Christ Gods which do not impose their will on others and are totally unconditional.

So, we as Christ Gods (and if you were drawn to this book, you are most likely a Christ God) respect others by not imposing our will on them and we practice unconditional love or at least as humans we attempt to. Evil gods are always attempting to control others for their own benefit and when they give something they always want something in return. We, as Christ Gods, are in integration or without judgment. Evil gods operate in total judgment, making rewards and punishments.

As Christ Gods, we didn't incarnate on this planet empty handed. We knew just how rough it would be for us here and so we arrived with a support team. Some of us see this team as guardian angels and spirit guides. They are all Christ Gods that are part of your personal support legion. They manifest in whatever form your beliefs allow. Since most of us believe in angels and spirit guides, that is how they manifest before us.

Years ago, I told a student that she had a fleet of ships of which she was in command. Up here in Mt. Shasta, many ships appear in the form of clouds that are round in shape and actually look similar to starships. She really could not accept that and I understood. She departed for San Jose a few days later. As she got about one hundred miles away, she noticed a strange cloud on her left. What was even stranger was that the cloud was traveling at the same speed she was (over 70 miles per hour). This cloud followed her through every road and turn all the way to San Jose, many hundreds of miles and hours later.

Clouds follow the winds. Winds don't follow the roads and rarely do the winds reach over seventy miles per hour on a clear sunny day. It was quite evident to her and me that this was not a cloud, but her personal starship. I have seen my own personal starship many times. The first time it appeared to me, it sent shakti (surges of energy) through my body to get my attention. From then on, I knew I was not alone.

We, as Christ Gods, have at our disposal, at our service and under our command our own legion of Christ Gods and fleet of starships. They are there primarily for our protection, but can perform other functions if necessary. If you are wondering why they do not assist us more, it is because of our Christ Directive which is not to impose our will on others. They must wait for a request or preferably a command. They are a major part of your realm.

Your personal legion and fleet await your commands. They do not want, nor do they expect prayer or the use of "please" or "thank you". They know who you are and what their duties are and are expecting and awaiting your commands. They respect, love and honor you for incarnating on this planet. If you feel comfortable with gratitude, that is fine, but it is totally unnecessary. As a God, before you were born, you set up a set of laws for them to follow. These laws were superseded by other laws at the time of your birth. This is a problem we all have had to contend with. That is why signing these laws is so important. They will reinstate most of the laws you had written before your birth and repeal those detrimental to you.

Our mission, as Christ Gods, is to liberate this planet from the control of evil gods. To do this, we must be in a human body. We do not have to physically go into battle with them. We just have to be here on the planet. Our Christ God aspect is doing the rest. The evil gods are trying their best to remove us from the planet and make our lives as miserable as possible.

I discovered that these beings cause much of the pain and suffering in our lives through possession. I proved it by depossessing myself and others. The result was an experience of relief of the pain. Because of this discovery, I made laws addressing these evil beings and evil gods a priority. It has been suggested that if you do not focus on these beings, they will not be attracted to you. This may work for those humans that are tourists on this planet, but for those of us who are here to liberate this planet and transform it, our intentions will attract the dark forces everytime.

My friend became very suicidal. After all attempts by me to depossess her, I took her to my friend who is a Native American shaman. He pulled quite a few beings out of her and immediately she stopped being suicidal. This occurred before the advent of the personal laws. Once she signed her personal laws, keeping those evil beings out of her body became easier.

One of the laws in the personal laws prohibits evil gods from imposing their will on us. For the most part, this law will keep us free from possession. I have been asked if that means that we do not have to depossess ourselves. That is not true. What the law does is make it easier to depossess ourselves with a command and keeps most of those unwanted beings out of our realms. I suggest that we all do the depossession command several times a day (God, deposses me now!). Do it now!

Signing laws and doing depossessions on ourselves daily is not what I call having fun. I know we would rather spend our time in nature experiencing the joys of simplicity, I know I would, but we came here to liberate this planet and when we are finished with our work, we can return to nature.

Another law mandates our income be over a certain amount per month. This does not create that income, but removes any laws and other blocks to that amount of income. You may still have to make some effort to create it, but it won't be as much an effort as before the laws.

From birth on, we have accepted many laws into our consciousness that are harmful and detrimental and even dangerous to us. One of the most important laws effectively repeals and makes null and void these harmful laws as well as all other laws contrary to the laws in the Personal Laws document.

Do not expect the laws to be a cure-all. They are very powerful, but still require some effort on our part to make commands and live our lives as Gods. As with all healing modalities, results will vary from person to person. The most important message of this book is not about the miracle healing effects of the Personal Laws, but that WE ARE GODS and must begin acting like Gods.

Being a God is a given for us. We were always Gods. Undoing our disempowering belief systems and retaking command of our lives will take some effort. All our lives, we were taught how to live as victims, human sheep with little power and little hope. This teaching became a habit for us. We ask God for things and thank God for things and pray for things and hope things will go okay for us. It is important that we change our habits.

It will be easier to change your habits if you are using this book with others. Once you have agreed to do this with friends or family, listen to each other as you speak and catch all those disempowering expressions. Anytime we pray, hope or wish for something, we are using disempowering expressions. When you hear this, tell the person and if requested, suggest a command that a God would say. Remember that Gods use commands. If you are doing this solo, then practice listening to yourself, catch yourself and give yourself commands to use instead. Sample commands are as follows:

1. I command the weather to be sunny and warm tomorrow.
2. I command my child, co-workers, parents, students to honor, respect and do as I ask.
3. I command that I am healed/that my friend is healed.
4. I command all my students to enjoy and benefit greatly form this seminar.

THE LAWS AND ASTROLOGY

When we are born, we take on a law that is like a pilot filing a flight plan or a vacationer planning an itinerary. It is your life plan per astrological energies and beliefs. Your life is held to this until you sign the personal laws. At that time your astrological influences are nullified and you are on your own to plan and change your life as you wish.

You can do this by writing your own laws using the pages titled "Amendments to the personal laws of _____".
Write these laws as you would write your itinerary. Be specific as to time, place, names, shapes, temperatures, quantities, etc..

Remember that you are a Christ God and your primary mission takes top priority. Once your primary mission is completed, expect all your laws to manifest. Until then, they will always manifest, if possible, and only when it doesn't compromise the mission.

TAKING THE LAWS TO THE WORLD

I have wanted to go to hospitals with these laws and offer them to each patient, but the logistics of that is more than I can handle. Even though the laws seem to be more effective when signed by the person than when signed on behalf of that person, I feel it is important that these laws be signed on behalf of as many people as possible. My objective is to reach the hundredth monkey effect. After a certain amount of people sign the laws or have the laws signed on their behalf, automatically these laws will apply to ALL HUMANS on the planet. This will create a major shift in mass consciousness that will benefit all mankind. For more information about the hundredth monkey effect, read The Hundredth Monkey by Ken Keyes.

I have begun to do this by offering free healing and help to everyone. Anyone can do this. I wrote a letter to the editor of my local newspaper offering free healings and help to everyone. All I asked was for them to write their name and the names of their children (if they wanted healings for them) on a sheet of paper and put it in an envelope and mail it to me. To maintain confidentiality, I asked that they do not put a return address on or in the envelope. Wanting to keep it as pure as possible, I asked nothing in return; not even any feedback. I put the letter on the internet also.

A copy of this letter is in the back of this book. You can find a copy of the Web page letter at:

> http://home.inreach.com/joybook/healing.html

When I began receiving names of those requesting healing and help, I took a set of laws and wrote at the top, "The personal laws of all persons named on the attached pages". I signed the laws "on their behalf". When I would receive pages with names on them, I would then attach them to that set of signed laws.

Anyone can do this. Just follow my lead. Write a letter to the editor of your local newspaper and process the letters in the same way. The results from the laws vary as with all spiritual healings, but since they are free and it is so simple to do, it is worth the effort. I feel that if one person out of one hundred benefits (and I know it is greater than that) it is well worth the effort.

These laws are augmentative. They assist all other healing modalities. They also cut all ties between us and any harmful beings we may have made contracts with in the past. It effects the removal of implants, repeals detrimental laws, removes limitations and much more.

I assist other healers and teachers in their work by asking their permission to do healing work on their clients and students. When they give me permission, all I do is take a set of laws and write at the top, "The personal laws of all the patients and clients of Doctor Jane Smith" or "The personal laws of all the students of Professor Jones". I actually phoned the chief physician of a childrens' hospital and asked if I could do healing work on all their patients. He gave me his permission. So, I took a set of laws and wrote, "The personal laws of all patients, past, present and future of the Blah Blah Blah Childrens' Hospital".

This works because permission to do healing work can pass from the client or patient to the healer to any other healer with that healer's permission or request. Since teachers effect a change in the student, they technically are healers also.

If you use the internet for Email, you can put a signature at the bottom of your Email messages that says:

For a free healing, click here:
http://home.inreach.com/joybook/healing.html

16

On that web page is a short letter, similar to the one I publish in letters to the editor columns. In it, I offer free healings unconditionally to all who apply. The only difference is that people respond by Email. I will do the rest. If you want, you can copy that web page, make it your own personal web page, change the reply addresses and have them send you the requests.

When you receive healing requests via Email, take a set of personal laws and write, "The personal laws of all named on the attached pages". Write, "On their behalf" above the signature line and sign your name and date it. Then, print out each Email message you get requesting a healing and attach it by a large paper clip to that set of laws. If you have your own healing modalities, just command that these people receive them also. You do not have to take any actions other than that.

MAKING YOUR OWN LAWS

Once you have signed your set of laws, you have laid down the foundation for all laws you wish to enact for the benefit and command of your own personal realm. Laws can be added to your original personal laws document as amendments. Just write at the top of a page, "Amendments to the personal laws of Jane Doe". Of course, use your name in place of Jane's and write all the laws you want under that title. Sign and date the page at the bottom. Keep it with the original set of personal laws and keep them all in a safe place.

Writing the laws is fairly simple. Read the laws I have written in the personal laws. Use their format as an example of how to write new laws. Affirmations are actually laws that are written daily. To make an affirmation a law, write it in an amendment document and sign it. Be very specific.

Laws can be written in affirmation form, mandate form, prohibition form and specification form. You will find the first three in the personal laws. Specifications laws are written to simplify our daily routine. For example, if you meditate every morning and make a whole list of requests or commands including protection, you can put all these requests, commands and protections in one specification and name them. You can name the specification anything. You can use a number, code name, or simple name. Lets say you call the specification, "morning meditation one".

You then write the law as follows:

Amendments to the personal laws of jane doe
Specification: Whenever I say or command, "morning meditation one", the following commands are to be implemented and maintained throughout the day or for twenty four hours:
1. God, deposses me now and maintain me free of possession!
2. Move me into a deep meditative state immediately and maintain me in that state for 45 minutes.
3. Integrate all suppressed patterns of energy in my body instantaneously and continuously.
4. Resolve all problems indicated in my dream state.

Signed _____ Date _____

Once you have done this, every morning meditation or ritual is simplified and accelerated. Just get out of bed, sit down and say, "I command morning meditation one". Everything will click in place. You can do this for every event in your life. You can do it to speed up and simplify your healing work you do on others. All groups of commands can be made into specifications where one word or group of words can put a whole group of commands into effect. I suggest the use of uncommon words, names or phrases. You can call them healing command one, two, three, etc.. You can call them headache healing, back pain healing, opening of the heart healing, etc..

You can make specifications that will command your God-self or subconscious to do certain specific tasks. Anything you can do, your subconscious can do.

I have put a set of personal laws in this book for you. Write all the names you ever used in this life at the top of the document and sign your present name at the bottom and date it. If you haven't done it already, I recommend you do it now.

GETTING THESE LAWS TO THE WORLD
To assist you in getting this important work to the world, I have put sets of laws in the back of this book for that purpose. One set is for all your students and clients and patients. Sign it and all your students, clients and patients will receive their benefits.

One set is for hospitals. Speak with the chief physician at your favorite hospital(s) and ask if you can do healing work on their patients. Ensure them that what you do is totally confidential, requires nothing on the hospitals part except for them giving you the okay. Once you have permission, write in the name of the hospital at the top of the laws and sign and date it at the bottom.

One set is for those applying for healing and help from a letter to the editor. Copy and send the letter to newspapers and magazines (located in the back of the book) putting your name and address where mine is. As you receive the letters, attach them to the set of laws titled, "The Personal Laws of all Persons Named on the Attached Pages". Don't forget to sign and date that set of laws.

One is for all the clients, patients and students of other healers or teachers. Offer to do free healings for clients, patients and students of other healers (doctors included) or teachers. Once they give you the okay, write their name on a sheet of paper and attach it to a signed set of laws titled, "The Personal Laws of all Students and Clients of the Healers/Teachers named on the Attached Pages".

Some have asked me why this is all possible. Anyone asking for a healing or is a student is asking for their life to be changed in some way. Unless they specifically limit the practitioner in how they must do it, they can use any method available. That includes using the personal laws.

MAKING COMMANDS

As a God on this planet at this time, it is important to simplify our lives. We can meditate and visualize what we want and we can do rituals and this is all fun stuff, but uses valuable time. It is also unnecessary. Whatever we, as Gods, want can be created either by a law or a command or by the combination of laws and commands. Sometimes it also requires some physical effort, but coupled with laws and commands, effort is reduced considerably.

The first command I recommend is: God, deposses me now! I have found that there are many nuisance beings in this world and the best way to deal with them is with that simple command. I recommend you do it at least four times a day.

Other commands can be for just about everything. In the past, I used to ask God for a parking space with time on the parking meter. Now, I command it. When I go shopping for food, I command no lines at the checkout counter when I am ready to leave. Sometimes, I must go into a building that may have nasty beings. I command a security team to go in and clear it out and secure it for me. If you get stopped by a police officer, command that the officer lets you go without giving you a summons. If you send out a letter or mailing, command that everyone responds quickly and positively. You can also make this a law. Laws can be for temporary events and permanent long term events. Commands are usually for temporary events. Practice making and using both. Use this book and teach it to others.

It is not necessary for you or anyone to read and/or understand or believe these laws for them to work. All that is necessary is for your name to be on them with your signature at the bottom. I strive for simplicity in my healing work. Please do not make these laws more complex than they are. I put the complexity in the laws so that our lives could be simpler and more effortless and pleasurable.

Knowledge can be the key to the Universe IF it is applied in a practical manner. Knowledge for the sake of knowing something is useless and counter-productive. Taking that knowledge and using it to construct a new world for yourself and others is pro-productive. As this applies to the laws and commands, when we understand how something works or operates, we can make laws and commands that are specific and hence very effective.

Knowing how our bodies work and using that knowledge to make laws and commands to effect changes is the quickest way of healing ourselves and others. Convert what you do to heal yourself and others into a group of commands and/or laws. When someone asks for a healing, just say the command word that defines those group of commands and they will be accomplished immediately and effortlessly.

Say you are an acupressure practitioner and your client has symptoms to address. By touching specific points on your clients body, you stimulate these points and effect a healing.

By specifying in writing what points are to be stimulated for each problem, giving that group of points a command name, and mandating that your Godself stimulate those specific points for a certain period of time any time you use that command name while touching your client or by naming the client. This can also be used with Reiki, and any other forms of healing.

THIS BOOK IS YOUR PERSONAL LAWS DOCUMENT

I have designed this book to be your personal document of personal laws. If you have not already signed the laws, go to the set of personal laws, write all the names you have used in this lifetime at the top and sign your present name at the bottom and date it. Remember that this is an important document and is to be kept in a safe and secure place.

Some people experience a discomfort for up to 72 hours after signing the laws. This is normal as your whole consciousness is being rebuilt and reorganized and any beings, creatures, devices, etc. that are not for your benefit are being removed and damage is being repaired.

Once you have done that, take any and all affirmations that you use and write them on the first page titled, "Amendments to the personal laws of_____". In the blank space at the top, write your present name only and sign and date it with your present name at the bottom.
Read through the laws to get an idea of how to word future laws you want to write. Be very specific when you write new laws. Don't assume anything!

Once you have signed your laws into effect, you may feel change taking place and, as with when you signed the original set of personal laws, things may be unsettled for a few days. If, after signing amendments, you experience major discomfort or pain, write the word "REPEALED" over the amendment in question and command that whatever was done by that law is to be undone. Things should settle down after that.

Once the smoke has cleared, examine the law you wrote to see just what element of it is causing a problem. Ask for guidance. Sometimes there is no problem with the way you wrote the law. Sometimes what you wrote is so effective and so on target that it enrages many evil gods who attempt retaliation. If this is the problem, command "Deposses protocol". That should take care of them.

I recommend that you get a copy of "The God Book" for each family member and have them sign the laws. If you have very young children, sign the laws on their behalf. When they are older and more receptive to this system of empowerment, show them the book and have them sign it for themselves. By then, you should be an expert on making laws. Teach them how to write their own.

If you have a parent under your care or others under your care and/or guardianship, get copies of the book for them also and sign the laws on their behalf.

COMMAND SUBCONSCIOUS PROGRAMS
In the laws, it mentions Command Subconscious Programs. They are automatically installed in your consciousness when you sign the laws. To learn more about the Command Subconscious Programs and their benefits, read The Joy Book. I recommend you use the Command Subconscious Programs in combination with your laws and commands. Basically, they reprogram your consciousness effortlessly, similar to how affirmations do, except it happens faster. They automatically integrate all contrary responses and they do it without any effort on your part.

PROOF THAT WE ARE GODS

This book is practical proof that we are Gods. In the personal laws, it states that we are Gods of our own realms. The personal laws also have laws that when signed do make a change in our lives. If we were not Gods, then signing the laws would do absolutely nothing. The fact that signing the laws creates a change in our lives is living proof that we are Gods and you can take that to the bank.

As with all books I have published, I rely on word of mouth for the books to "get out there in the world". So, please tell all your friends about this book and if you are a spiritual teacher, make it recommended reading for all your students.

If you want to share your experiences you have with signing the laws and using this book, please send your letters to me. If they require an answer, please send a self addressed and stamped envelope. If you do not mind if your letter be published as a testimonial, please say so in your letter. Unless you give me your permission, I treat all letters as confidential.

PREVIOUSLY SIGNED ON YOUR BEHALF

When I discovered the power and importance of these laws, I asked my guidance if I could sign them on behalf of everyone. I was told to sign a set on behalf of all humans and on behalf of all my students. I am not sure if these signings took effect for everyone, but it may have for you. If that is so, you may not get much of an initial shift when you sign them now. Just know that they are in effect for you and working in your life.

Remember, signing these laws is only one way for you to exercise your God powers. Writing your own laws in the form of amendments is another very important way. Don't forget to write your own laws.

The

Personal

Laws

of the

God

known as

_____

(your name here)

The Personal Laws of

_____
_____
_____
_____
_____
_____
_____
_____
_____
_____
_____
_____

1. I proclaim that I am the Lord, God, King (Queen) of my realm and domain. All Christ Gods under my command have full authority to enforce the laws in this document. Christ Gods are all mandated to obey and enforce all the laws in this document always and they have the authority to make all commands, authorities and responsibilities and creations necessary to enforce these laws. All Christ Gods have my full authority to act on my behalf in enforcing all of my laws, commands and specifications. All evil gods (anti-Christs) are prohibited from entering my realm and domain or effecting it or me in any way.

2. It is prohibited for command authority and/or authority to make and repeal and change laws to transfer from me to any other being by touch or physical contact in any way shape or form (This is a very common way for problems to occur). Any and all command authority and authority to make and repeal and change laws by other than me is now rescinded, repealed and null and void and any laws,

commands, authorities, responsibilities made by previous transfers are now repealed, rescinded, null and void. This law does not apply to Global Christ Laws.

3. All laws, paradigms, thoughts, thought forms, structures, beings, creatures, and implants contrary to the laws in this document and all amendment documents are repealed, dissolved, destroyed, null, and void forevermore now and as new laws are created by me.

4. It is prohibited for any god, entity, being, creature, and/or entity to possess any of my bodies.

5. All treaties, covenants, conventions and vows between me and all Gods, entities, beings and humans are hereby repealed, null, void and canceled. All rights, laws and other legal documents, contracts, agreements made by or from the authorities given by these treaties and vows are also repealed, canceled, null and void.

6. Laws can only be created, altered and/or revoked by me and only when I am awake typing or writing them in a document and then signing them or in the case of these laws, just by signing them. It is prohibited for any laws to be made, changed or revoked during the time when I am sleeping or meditating or any time when I am not fully awake or by any other Gods. It is prohibited for any god to make commands or laws while in my bodies.

7. It is prohibited for any God, being or entity to alter, corrupt, or make less effective or less beneficial any and all of my Command Subconscious Programs, if installed. It is also prohibited for the aforementioned to write protect my consciousness or prevent the installation or full effectiveness of all Command Subconscious Programs and their ability to erase and write beliefs, thoughts, commands, paradigms

and other bytes of information in my consciousness.

8. Communications is to be establish and maintain between me and all Christ Gods. It is prohibited for the aforementioned communications to be interfered with or blocked in any way, shape or form by any god or being.

9. All the laws in this document are spelled out and defined. If somehow these laws get undone, I can put into full effectivity all these laws anytime anywhere by simply saying "I COMMAND MY LAWS". (Recommended once a day) When the aforementioned command is said, only those laws printed in the third dimension and signed by me are to be enforced. Any and all laws imbedded in a stealthy way are not valid and are to be ignored and removed from the document.

10. Touching me, being in my presence, in my energy field, exchanging energy in no way can transfer authority for the purpose of making, changing or repealing laws and or commands. All beings, Gods and/or entities in my energy field are prohibited from making, modifying, changing, and/or repealing laws, commands, authorities, responsibilities.

11. My other God aspects have permission and authority to effect all third dimensional Gods including those challenging me and in my third dimensional bodies and other bodies, to wit, full authority to use all Christ God defensive protocols. Any laws prohibiting this does not apply to this.

12. Any imposition on and/or restriction of my total freedom is prohibited.

13. It is mandated that all Christ Gods under my command have the authority to interact with and effect change in the third dimension for the purposes of enforcing all the laws in this document.

14. It is mandated that full armor is created and maintained around my human body, God body, vehicles and living quarters that is impervious to all attacks and infiltrations. Enforcement of this law is a top priority. This law cannot block my love flow. (It has been found that beings, including humans, have the ability to send hostile energy to us. This blocks it)

15. PRIORITIES: I mandate and make law the following priorities. First priority is to protect me, and all of my aspects. This includes my human bodies and all of my God bodies and my consciousness. This includes maintaining a fortress, armor, shield and bunker around my body and living quarters. This includes the removal and prevention of all evil portals, wayportals, vortexes, anchors, implants and any other devices or energies or creations within the aforementioned shields, bunkers, fortresses, armor and my bodies. Priority two is to enforce all my laws and commands and carry them out to completion as appropriate.

16. All Christ Gods under my command and allied to me and the Gods under my command have full authority and permission to interact, and effect third dimensional gods as well as gods in all other dimensions and time continuums and space and planes of existence.

17. The energies in my bodies are to be flowing unrestricted and uncontrolled. Any restriction of my energies by me or anyone else is prohibited. All laws prohibiting the unrestricted flow of my energies are repealed.

18. It is prohibited for me to have anything else other than perfect health and a perfect body. It is mandated that my body always experiences perfect health and be the exact weight and dimensions I specify consciously.

19. Any laws causing me to experience fear, pain, illnesses, disabilities, struggle, lack of power and/or energy, lack of joy, lack of money, lack of prosperity are hereby repealed and all structures and thought forms and paradigms created by them or associated with them are dissolved. (This does not effect normal pain sensations or grieving.)

20. It is mandated that I source my God being for 100% of my nutrition and energy and source food and other sources for my 0% source of nutrition and energy. It is mandated that I source myself for all my unconditional love and approval. When it comes to unconditional love and approval, I am the main meal (source) and everyone else is the dessert. (As a God, one does not require food and can source their own Godself for energy and nutrition.)

21. I command that all beings love, honor and respect me unconditionally and that I do the same with them and myself.

22. It is mandated that all links and connections between me and all humans, gods and other beings are severed. (this is a very important law. When the laws were first developed, a few healers experienced major incursions through their connection with their students and clients. When this law was added, the problem stopped immediately.) It is prohibited for me to have links and connections with humans, gods and other beings except for love or healing purposes and then, they are to be severed immediately after the healing is consciously completed or when I leave the client's presence. All laws mandating links and the maintenance of links between me and other humans are repealed. (This does not prohibit conscious connections with the ones you love provided it is agreed upon by both parties and is only momentary.)

23. It is prohibited for me to be addicted to any substance and/or experience. All laws creating addiction are repealed.
24. It is mandated that my body is immune and impervious to all toxins, poisons, viruses, bacteria and parasites
25. It is prohibited for all viruses, parasites and detrimental organisms to trespass or exist in or on my bodies and/or my bodies to experience illness or disability in any form including allergies.
26. All laws in this document are superior to all laws of all governments in the world.
27. It is prohibited for me or anyone else to experience harmful effects from touching and loving and healing others.
28. It is prohibited for me to judge anything or anyone, or perceive them as "good", "bad", "right", or "wrong".
29. It is prohibited for others to judge me or perceive me as "good", "bad", "right", or "wrong".
30. It is mandated that I am always undedicated from evil and totally dedicated to the Christ.
31. It is prohibited for me to have any contracts, covenants, vows or agreements with evil gods or beings. Any that are in existence are hereby and forever more canceled, null and void without consequence.
32. It is mandated that I have all my Christ God powers and abilities and the full authority, knowledge and ability to use them. I understand that they will appear when I have learned to use them.
33. All Gods are to respect and obey the laws in this document fully. Any and all Gods violating or attempting to violate any of the laws in this document are to immediately experience full integration back into the source.

34. It is mandated that all patterns of energy in my bodies be integrated at a rate that is 1000 times greater than the rate of activation and/or creation of those patterns of energy at all times.
35. My will is my own. It is prohibited for any other being, creature, god to impose their will on me or for me to give my will to another being, creature or god.
36. It is mandated that the Empowerment, Safe, and Joy Command Subconscious Programs are installed and operational in my consciousness. All Command Subconscious Programs are to be protected and maintained per Global Christ Laws. (Read The Joy Book for more information on these programs)
37. It is mandated that the only way that these laws and any amendments to these laws can be repealed and/or canceled is by me physically tearing up this document or by me personally writing the word "REPEALED" on top of the specific law or amendment and signing and dating it. In no way can the use of drugs, alcohol, the sexual act or any act effect the validity and enforceability of these laws and/or amendments.
38. Anywhere in this document where it refers to evil gods, it also refers to and applies to evil entities.
39. It is mandated that my body are maintained free of toxins, poisons, and heavy metals.
40. It is prohibited for any implants to be installed, maintained and/or remain within my body. It is mandated that all implants be removed from my body.
41. It is mandated that all organs, glands, systems and the immune systems of my body function as originally designed in full health.

42. It is mandated that my body be maintained free of all cancerous growths and other harmful organisms and in perfect health unconditionally.

43. Karma is prohibited in my life experience. Any and all laws mandating karma are now repealed.

44. It is mandated that I am immortal and live forever. It is mandated that I youth to the age of 21-26 years old. It is prohibited for me to age. It is prohibited for me to die. (This does not prohibit you from choosing death or aging at any time.)

45. It is prohibited for anyone else to be responsible for my happiness. I am totally responsible for my happiness.

46. It is prohibited for me to have less than (write an amount here or default is $1,000,000) $_____ a month net income. It is mandated that my income is always over $_____ a month net (default is $1,000,000). It is mandated that that I always have more than what I require.

47. It is mandated that the primary source of my energy is the excess fat cells in my body. It is prohibited for food ingested in my body to be used for the creation of fat cells.

48. It is mandated that the my Godself affect any and all healings, repairs, modifications, changes, and/or reprogramming necessary to return to me my full health, vitality, God powers and prosperity. All structures, paradigms, belief systems created by evil gods are to be removed immediately. This is a top priority law.

49. It is mandated that my body and consciousness be scanned hourly for potential problems, illnesses, disorders, implants, and damage and that any that is discovered is to be healed, repaired, reversed, removed and neutralized immediately. It is also

mandated that command subconscious programs be retrieved as part of the healing responses.

50. It is mandated that all self sabotage systems, programming, devices, entities, beings, creatures, gods and/or beliefs within my body, consciousness, mind, energy field be dissolved, destroyed, removed, erased now and forever permanently. It is prohibited for me to have any self sabotage systems, programming, devices, entities, beings, creatures, gods and/or beliefs within my body, consciousness, mind, energy field.

Signed_____

Date _____

Amendments to the Personal Laws of

_____
(your current name here)

_____

_____

_____

_____

_____

_____

_____

_____

_____

_____

_____

_____

_____

_____

Signature _____ Date _____
(your current name here)

Amendments to the Personal Laws of

_____
(your current name here)

_____

_____

_____

_____

_____

_____

_____

_____

_____

_____

_____

_____

_____

_____

Signature _____ Date _____
(your current name here)

Amendments to the Personal Laws of

_____
(your current name here)

_____

_____

_____

_____

_____

_____

_____

_____

_____

_____

_____

_____

_____

_____

_____

_____

Signature _____ Date _____
(your current name here)

Amendments to the Personal Laws of

_____
(your current name here)

_____

_____

_____

_____

_____

_____

_____

_____

_____

_____

_____

_____

_____

_____

_____

_____

_____

Signature _____ Date _____
(your current name here)

Amendments to the Personal Laws of

_____
(your current name here)

_____

_____

_____

_____

_____

_____

_____

_____

_____

_____

_____

_____

_____

_____

_____

Signature _____ Date _____
(your current name here)

Amendments to the Personal Laws of

_____
(your current name here)

_____

_____

_____

_____

_____

_____

_____

_____

_____

_____

_____

_____

_____

_____

_____

_____

_____

Signature _____ Date _____
(your current name here)

Amendments to the Personal Laws of

_____

(your current name here)

_____

_____

_____

_____

_____

_____

_____

_____

_____

_____

_____

_____

_____

_____

_____

_____

_____

Signature _____ Date _____

(your current name here)

Amendments to the Personal Laws of

_____
(your current name here)

_____
_____
_____
_____
_____
_____
_____
_____
_____
_____
_____
_____
_____
_____
_____
_____
_____
_____
_____

Signature _____ Date _____
(your current name here)

42

Amendments to the Personal Laws of

_____
(your current name here)

_____

_____

_____

_____

_____

_____

_____

_____

_____

_____

_____

_____

_____

_____

_____

Signature _____ Date _____
(your current name here)

Amendments to the Personal Laws of

_____
(your current name here)

_____

_____

_____

_____

_____

_____

_____

_____

_____

_____

_____

_____

_____

_____

_____

_____

Signature _____ Date _____
(your current name here)

Amendments to the Personal Laws of

_____
(your current name here)

_____
_____
_____
_____
_____
_____
_____
_____
_____
_____
_____
_____
_____
_____
_____
_____
_____

Signature _____ Date _____
(your current name here)

USING AFFIRMATIONS AS LAWS

The document below is an example of how one can write an amendment document using common affirmations.

Amendments to the Personal Laws of

_____

(Line through all laws that do not apply to you and fill in all blank spaces)

1. I forgive myself for everything.
2. I am innocent.
3. I am forgiven.
4. I compare everything only to itself.
5. I am free from judgment.
6. I am free from guilt
7. I am overflowing with love and money.
8. I am without fear.
9. I am acquited of all guilt now and forever
10. I am pardoned now and forever
11. I am redeemed now and forever
12. I am a God
13. Change is safe, easy, effortless and joyful for me
14. I am absolved of all guilt now and forever
15. I am at peace with the world and the world is at peace with me
16. My life experience on Earth is one of ease and joy.
17. My body metabolism adjusts instantly to maintain my ideal weight of _____ pounds
18. I am now my perfect weight of _____ pounds
19. I now weigh _____ pounds
20. All excess water flows freely from my body
21. I am free of excess water
22. I am free of excess fat tissue
23. My emotions flow freely and joyfully.
24. I love my body

46

25. I love being in my body
26. I want to be here now
27. I am invincible
28. I am immune to attack
29. I have superior strength and agility
30. I am safe with all men
31. I am safe with all women
32. I am in total control of my body and life now
33. All my energies and emotions integrate instantaneously and joyfully
34. I love myself unconditionally
35. I forgive my mommy and daddy for everything
36. I am successful at everything I do
37. Food is safe, pleasurable and healthy for me
38. I can say no and still be loved unconditionally
39. I deserve to be happy
40. I have the power to succeed in everything I do
41. I love my body unconditionally
42. When in fear, I breathe fully, freely and circularly
43. I now integrate emotions instantly
44. It is safe for me to be alone
45. I am safe when I am alone
46. I am always safe
47. I integrate anger instantly, effortlessly and joyfully
48. I integrate rage instantly, effortlessly and joyfully
49. It is safe for me to express all my emotions
50. Everything is perfect and so is everything else.
51. I am overflowing with love and money.
52. I am without fear.
53. Whatever I consciously command manifests instantly.
54. I deserve to receive whatever I consciously command.
55. Change is safe, easy and effortless and joyful for me
56. I only become pregnant when I consciously choose to be pregnant

57. I am in full conscious control of my sexual experiences
58. I am strong, powerful and invincible
59. I attract money easily and effortlessly
60. I now have more money than I can possibly spend, save, give away or lose
61. I am overflowing with love and money.
62. I am without fear.

Signed_____
(your current name here)

Date _____

The Personal Laws of all my students, clients and patients

1.   I proclaim that I am the Lord, God, King (Queen) of my realm and domain. All Christ Gods under my command have full authority to enforce the laws in this document. Christ Gods are all mandated to obey and enforce all the laws in this document always and they have the authority to make all commands, authorities and responsibilities and creations necessary to enforce these laws. All Christ Gods have my full authority to act on my behalf in enforcing all of my laws, commands and specifications. All evil gods (anti-Christs) are prohibited from entering my realm and domain or effecting it or me in any way.

2.   It is prohibited for command authority and/or authority to make and repeal and change laws to transfer from me to any other being by touch or physical contact in any way shape or form (This is a very common way for problems to occur). Any and all command authority and authority to make and repeal and change laws by other than me is now rescinded, repealed and null and void and any laws, commands, authorities, responsibilities made by previous transfers are now repealed, rescinded, null and void. This law does not apply to Global Christ Laws.

3.   All laws, paradigms, thoughts, thought forms, structures, beings, creatures, and implants contrary to the laws in this document and all amendment documents are repealed, dissolved, destroyed, null, and void forevermore now and as new laws are created by me.

4.   It is prohibited for any god, entity, being, creature, and/or entity to possess any of my bodies.

5.   All treaties, covenants, conventions and vows between me and all Gods, entities, beings and humans are hereby repealed, null, void and canceled. All rights, laws and other legal documents, contracts, agreements made by or from the authorities given by these treaties and vows are also repealed, canceled, null and void.

6.   Laws can only be created, altered and/or revoked by me and only when I am awake typing or writing them in a document and then signing them or in the case of these laws, just by signing them. It is prohibited for any laws to be made, changed or revoked during the time when I am sleeping or meditating or any time when I am not fully awake or by any other Gods. It is prohibited for any god to make commands or laws while in my bodies.

7.   It is prohibited for any God, being or entity to alter, corrupt, or make less effective or less beneficial any and all of my Command Subconscious Programs, if installed. It is also prohibited for the aforementioned to write protect my consciousness or prevent the installation or full effectiveness of all Command Subconscious Programs and their ability to erase and write beliefs, thoughts, commands, paradigms and other bytes of information in my consciousness.

8.   Communications is to is establish and maintain between me and all Christ Gods. It is prohibited for the aforementioned communications to be interfered with or blocked in any way, shape or form by any god or being.

9.   All the laws in this document are spelled out and defined. If somehow these laws get undone, I can put into full effectivity all these laws anytime anywhere by simply saying "I COMMAND MY LAWS". (Recommended once a day) When the aforementioned command is said, only those laws printed in the third dimension and signed by me are to be enforced. Any and all laws imbedded in a stealthy way are not valid and are to be ignored and removed from the document.

10.   Touching me, being in my presence, in my energy field, exchanging energy in no way can transfer authority for the purpose of making, changing or repealing laws and or commands. All beings, Gods and/or entities in my energy field are prohibited from making, modifying, changing, and/or repealing laws, commands, authorities, responsibilities.

11.   My other God aspects have permission and authority to effect all third dimensional Gods including those challenging me and in my third dimensional bodies and other bodies, to wit, full authority to use all Christ God defensive protocols. Any laws prohibiting this does not apply to this.

12.   Any imposition on and/or restriction of my total freedom is prohibited.

13.   It is mandated that all Christ Gods under my command have the authority to interact with and effect change in the third dimension for the purposes of enforcing all the laws in this document.

14.   It is mandated that full armor is created and maintained around my human body, God body, vehicles and living quarters that is impervious to all attacks and infiltrations. Enforcement of this law is a top priority. This law cannot block my love flow. (It has been found that beings, including humans, have the ability to send hostile energy to us. This blocks it)

15.   PRIORITIES: I mandate and make law the following priorities. First priority is to protect me, and all of my aspects. This includes my human bodies and all of my God bodies and my consciousness. This includes maintaining a fortress, armor, shield and bunker around my body and living quarters. This includes the removal and prevention of all evil portals, wayportals, vortexes, anchors, implants and any other devices or energies or creations within the aforementioned shields, bunkers, fortresses, armor and my bodies. Priority two is to enforce all my laws and commands and carry them out to completion as appropriate.

16.   All Christ Gods under my command and allied to me and the Gods under my command have full authority and permission to interact, and effect third dimensional gods as well as gods in all other dimensions and time continuums and space and planes of existence.

17.   The energies in my bodies are to be flowing unrestricted and uncontrolled. Any restriction of my energies by me or anyone else is prohibited. All laws prohibiting the unrestricted flow of my energies are repealed.

18.   It is prohibited for me to have anything else other than perfect health and a perfect body. It is mandated that my body always experiences perfect health and be the exact weight and dimensions I specify consciously.

19.   Any laws causing me to experience fear, pain, illnesses, disabilities, struggle, lack of power and/or energy, lack of joy, lack of money, lack of prosperity are hereby repealed and all structures and thought forms and paradigms created by them or associated with them are dissolved. (This does not effect normal pain sensations or grieving.)

20.   It is mandated that I source my God being for 100% of my nutrition and energy and source food and other sources for my 0% source of nutrition and energy. It is mandated that I source myself for all my unconditional love and approval. When it comes to unconditional love and approval, I am the main meal (source) and everyone else is the dessert. (As a God, one does not require food and can source their own Godself for energy and nutrition.)

21.   I command that all beings love, honor and respect me unconditionally and that I do the same with them and myself.

22.   It is mandated that all links and connections between me and all humans, gods and other beings are severed. (this is a very important law, when the laws were first developed, a few healers experienced major incursions through their connection with their students and clients. When this law was added, the problem stopped immediately.) It is prohibited for me to have links and connections with humans, gods and other beings except for love or healing purposes and then, they are to be severed immediately after the healing is consciously completed or when I leave the client's presence. All laws mandating links and the maintenance of links between me and other humans are repealed. (This does not prohibit conscious connections with the ones you love provided it is agreed upon by both parties and is only momentary.)

23.   It is prohibited for me to be addicted to any substance and/or experience. All laws creating addiction are repealed.

24.   It is mandated that my body is immune and impervious to all toxins, poisons, viruses, bacteria and parasites.

25.   It is prohibited for all viruses, parasites and detrimental organisms to trespass or exist in or on my bodies and/or my bodies to experience illness or disability in any form including allergies.

26.   All laws in this document are superior to all laws of all governments in the world.

27.   It is prohibited for me or anyone else to experience harmful effects from touching and loving and healing others.

28.   It is prohibited for me to judge anything or anyone, or perceive them as "good", "bad", "right", or "wrong".

29.   It is prohibited for others to judge me or perceive me as "good", "bad", "right", or "wrong".

30.   It is mandated that I am always undedicated from evil and totally dedicated to the Christ.

31.   It is prohibited for me to have any contracts, covenants, vows or agreements with evil gods or beings. Any that are in existence are hereby and forever more canceled, null and void without consequence.

32. It is mandated that I have all my Christ God powers and abilities and the full authority, knowledge and ability to use them. I understand that they will appear when I have learned to use them.
33. All Gods are to respect and obey the laws in this document fully. Any and all Gods violating or attempting to violate any of the laws in this document are to immediately experience full integration back into the source.
34. It is mandated that all patterns of energy in my bodies be integrated at a rate that is 1000 times greater than the rate of activation and/or creation of those patterns of energy at all times.
35. My will is my own. It is prohibited for any other being, creature, god to impose their will on me or for me to give my will to another being, creature or god.
36. It is mandated that the Empowerment, Safe, and Joy Command Subconscious Programs are installed and operational in my consciousness. All Command Subconscious Programs are to be protected and maintained per Global Christ Laws. (Read The Joy Book for more information on these programs)
37. It is mandated that the only way that these laws and any amendments to these laws can be repealed and/or canceled is by me physically tearing up this document or by me personally writing the word "REPEALED" on top of the specific law or amendment and signing and dating it. In no way can the use of drugs, alcohol, the sexual act or any act effect the validity and enforceability of these laws and/or amendments.
38. Anywhere in this document where it refers to evil gods, it also refers to and applies to evil entities.
39. It is mandated that my body are maintained free of toxins, poisons, and heavy metals.
40. It is prohibited for any implants to be installed, maintained and/or remain within my body. It is mandated that all implants be removed from my body.
41. It is mandated that all organs, glands, systems and the immune systems of my body function as originally designed in full health.
42. It is mandated that my body be maintained free of all cancerous growths and other harmful organisms and in perfect health unconditionally.
43. Karma is prohibited in my life experience. Any and all laws mandating karma are now repealed.
44. It is mandated that I am immortal and live forever. It is mandated that I youth to the age of 21-26 years old. It is prohibited for me to age. It is prohibited for me to die. (This does not prohibit you from choosing death or aging at any time.)
45. It is prohibited for anyone else to be responsible for my happiness. I am totally responsible for my happiness.
46. It is prohibited for me to have less than (write an amount here or default is $1,000,000) $_____ a month net income. It is mandated that my income is always over $_____ a month net (default is $1,000,000). It is mandated that that I always have more than what I require.
47. It is mandated that the primary source of my energy is the excess fat cells in my body. It is prohibited for food ingested in my body to be used for the creation of fat cells.
48. It is mandated that the my Godself affect any and all healings, repairs, modifications, changes, and/or reprogramming necessary to return to me my full health, vitality, God powers and prosperity. All structures, paradigms, belief systems created by evil gods are to be removed immediately. This is a top priority law.
49. It is mandated that my body and consciousness be scanned hourly for potential problems, illnesses, disorders, implants, and damage and that any that is discovered is to be healed, repaired, reversed, removed and neutralized immediately. It is also mandated that command subconscious programs are retrieved as part of the healing responses.
50. It is mandated that all self sabotage systems, programming, devices, entities, beings, creatures, gods and/or beliefs within my body, consciousness, mind, energy field be dissolved, destroyed, removed, erased now and forever permanently. It is prohibited for me to have any self sabotage systems, programming, devices, entities, beings, creatures, gods and/or beliefs within my body, consciousness, mind, energy field.

On their behalf,

Signed_____

(your current name here)

Date _____

The Personal Laws of all persons
named on the attached pages

1. I proclaim that I am the Lord, God, King (Queen) of my realm and domain. All Christ Gods under my command have full authority to enforce the laws in this document. Christ Gods are all mandated to obey and enforce all the laws in this document always and they have the authority to make all commands, authorities and responsibilities and creations necessary to enforce these laws. All Christ Gods have my full authority to act on my behalf in enforcing all of my laws, commands and specifications. All evil gods (anti-Christs) are prohibited from entering my realm and domain or effecting it or me in any way.

2. It is prohibited for command authority and/or authority to make and repeal and change laws to transfer from me to any other being by touch or physical contact in any way shape or form (This is a very common way for problems to occur). Any and all command authority and authority to make and repeal and change laws by other than me is now rescinded, repealed and null and void and any laws, commands, authorities, responsibilities made by previous transfers are now repealed, rescinded, null and void. This law does not apply to Global Christ Laws.

3. All laws, paradigms, thoughts, thought forms, structures, beings, creatures, and implants contrary to the laws in this document and all amendment documents are repealed, dissolved, destroyed, null, and void forevermore now and as new laws are created by me.

4. It is prohibited for any god, entity, being, creature, and/or entity to possess any of my bodies.

5. All treaties, covenants, conventions and vows between me and all Gods, entities, beings and humans are hereby repealed, null, void and canceled. All rights, laws and other legal documents, contracts, agreements made by or from the authorities given by these treaties and vows are also repealed, canceled, null and void.

6. Laws can only be created, altered and/or revoked by me and only when I am awake typing or writing them in a document and then signing them or in the case of these laws, just by signing them. It is prohibited for any laws to be made, changed or revoked during the time when I am sleeping or meditating or any time when I am not fully awake or by any other Gods. It is prohibited for any god to make commands or laws while in my bodies.

7. It is prohibited for any God, being or entity to alter, corrupt, or make less effective or less beneficial any and all of my Command Subconscious Programs, if installed. It is also prohibited for the aforementioned to write protect my consciousness or prevent the installation or full effectiveness of all Command Subconscious Programs and their ability to erase and write beliefs, thoughts, commands, paradigms and other bytes of information in my consciousness.

8. Communications is to be establish and maintain between me and all Christ Gods. It is prohibited for the aforementioned communications to be interfered with or blocked in any way, shape or form by any god or being.

9. All the laws in this document are spelled out and defined. If somehow these laws get undone, I can put into full effectivity all these laws anytime anywhere by simply saying "I COMMAND MY LAWS". (Recommended once a day) When the aforementioned command is said, only those laws printed in the third dimension and signed by me are to be enforced. Any and all laws imbedded in a stealthy way are not valid and are to be ignored and removed from the document.

10. Touching me, being in my presence, in my energy field, exchanging energy in no way can transfer authority for the purpose of making, changing or repealing laws and or commands. All beings, Gods and/or entities in my energy field are prohibited from making, modifying, changing, and/or repealing laws, commands, authorities, responsibilities.

11. My other God aspects have permission and authority to effect all third dimensional God including those challenging me and in my third dimensional bodies and other bodies, to wit, full authority to use all Christ God defensive protocols. Any laws prohibiting this does not apply to this.

12. Any imposition on and/or restriction of my total freedom is prohibited.

13. It is mandated that all Christ Gods under my command have the authority to interact with and effect change in the third dimension for the purposes of enforcing all the laws in this document.

14. It is mandated that full armor is created and maintained around my human body, God body, vehicles and living quarters that is impervious to all attacks and infiltrations. Enforcement of this law is a top priority. This law cannot block my love flow. (It has been found that beings, including humans, have the ability to send hostile energy to us. This blocks it)

15. PRIORITIES: I mandate and make law the following priorities. First priority is to protect me, and all of my aspects. This includes my human bodies and all of my God bodies and my consciousness. This includes maintaining a fortress, armor, shield and bunker around my body and living quarters. This includes the removal and prevention of all evil portals, wayportals, vortexes, anchors, implants and any other devices or energies or creations within the aforementioned shields, bunkers, fortresses, armor and my bodies. Priority two is to enforce all my laws and commands and carry them out to completion as appropriate.

16. All Christ Gods under my command and allied to me and the Gods under my command have full authority and permission to interact, and effect third dimensional gods as well as gods in all other dimensions and time continuums and space and planes of existence.

17. The energies in my bodies are to be flowing unrestricted and uncontrolled. Any restriction of my energies by me or anyone else is prohibited. All laws prohibiting the unrestricted flow of my energies are repealed.

18. It is prohibited for me to have anything else other than perfect health and a perfect body. It is mandated that my body always experiences perfect health and be the exact weight and dimensions I specify consciously.

19. Any laws causing me to experience fear, pain, illnesses, disabilities, struggle, lack of power and/or energy, lack of joy, lack of money, lack of prosperity are hereby repealed and all structures and thought forms and paradigms created by them or associated with them are dissolved. (This does not effect normal pain sensations or grieving.)

20. It is mandated that I source my God being for 100% of my nutrition and energy and source food and other sources for my 0% source of nutrition and energy. It is mandated that I source myself for all my unconditional love and approval. When it comes to unconditional love and approval. I am the main meal (source) and everyone else is the dessert. (As a God, one does not require food and can source their own Godself for energy and nutrition.)

21. I command that all beings love, honor and respect me unconditionally and that I do the same with them and myself.

22. It is mandated that all links and connections between me and all humans, gods and other beings are severed. (this is a very important law. when the laws were first developed, a few healers experienced major incursions through their connection with their students and clients. When this law was added, the problem stopped immediately.) It is prohibited for me to have links and connections with humans, gods and other beings except for love or healing purposes and then, they are to be severed immediately after the healing is consciously completed or when I leave the client's presence. All laws mandating links and the maintenance of links between me and other humans are repealed. (This does not prohibit conscious connections with the ones you love provided it is agreed upon by both parties and is only momentary.)

23. It is prohibited for me to be addicted to any substance and/or experience. All laws creating addiction are repealed.

24. It is mandated that my body is immune and impervious to all toxins, poisons, viruses, bacteria and parasites.

25. It is prohibited for all viruses, parasites and detrimental organisms to trespass or exist in or on my bodies and/or my bodies to experience illness or disability in any form including allergies.

26. All laws in this document are superior to all laws of all governments in the world.

27. It is prohibited for me or anyone else to experience harmful effects from touching and loving and healing others.

28. It is prohibited for me to judge anything or anyone, or perceive them as "good", "bad", "right", or "wrong".

29. It is prohibited for others to judge me or perceive me as "good", "bad", "right", or "wrong".

30. It is mandated that I am always undedicated from evil and totally dedicated to the Christ.

31. It is prohibited for me to have any contracts, covenants, vows or agreements with evil gods or beings. Any that are in existence are hereby and forever more canceled, null and void without consequence.

32. It is mandated that I have all my Christ God powers and abilities and the full authority, knowledge and ability to use them. I understand that they will appear when I have learned to use them.

33. All Gods are to respect and obey the laws in this document fully. Any and all Gods violating or attempting to violate any of the laws in this document are to immediately experience full integration back into the source.

34. It is mandated that all patterns of energy in my bodies be integrated at a rate that is 1000 times greater than the rate of activation and/or creation of those patterns of energy at all times.

35. My will is my own. It is prohibited for any other being, creature, god to impose their will on me or for me to give my will to another being, creature or god.

36. It is mandated that the Empowerment, Safe, and Joy Command Subconscious Programs are installed and operational in my consciousness. All Command Subconscious Programs are to be protected and maintained per Global Christ Laws. (Read The Joy Book for more information on these programs)

37. It is mandated that the only way that these laws and any amendments to these laws can be repealed and/or canceled is by me physically tearing up this document or by me personally writing the word "REPEALED" on top of the specific law or amendment and signing and dating it. In no way can the use of drugs, alcohol, the sexual act or any act effect the validity and enforceability of these laws and/or amendments.

38. Anywhere in this document where it refers to evil gods, it also refers to and applies to evil entities.

39. It is mandated that my body are maintained free of toxins, poisons, and heavy metals.

40. It is prohibited for any implants to be installed, maintained and/or remain within my body. It is mandated that all implants be removed from my body.

41. It is mandated that all organs, glands, systems and the immune systems of my body function as originally designed in full health.

42. It is mandated that my body be maintained free of all cancerous growths and other harmful organisms and in perfect health unconditionally.

43. Karma is prohibited in my life experience. Any and all laws mandating karma are now repealed.

44. It is mandated that I am immortal and live forever. It is mandated that I youth to the age of 21-26 years old. It is prohibited for me to age. It is prohibited for me to die. (This does not prohibit you from choosing death or aging at any time.)

45. It is prohibited for anyone else to be responsible for my happiness. I am totally responsible for my happiness.

46. It is prohibited for me to have less than (write an amount here or default is $1,000,000) $_____ a month net income. It is mandated that my income is always over $_____ a month net (default is $1,000,000). It is mandated that that I always have more than what I require.

47. It is mandated that the primary source of my energy is the excess fat cells in my body. It is prohibited for food ingested in my body to be used for the creation of fat cells.

48. It is mandated that the my Godself affect any and all healings, repairs, modifications, changes, and/or reprogramming necessary to return to me my full health, vitality, God powers and prosperity. All structures, paradigms, belief systems created by evil gods are to be removed immediately. This is a top priority law.

49. It is mandated that my body and consciousness be scanned hourly for potential problems, illnesses, disorders, implants, and damage and that any that is discovered is to be healed, repaired, reversed, removed and neutralized immediately. It is also mandated that command subconscious programs be retrieved as part of the healing responses.

50. It is mandated that all self sabotage systems, programming, devices, entities, beings, creatures, gods and/or beliefs within my body, consciousness, mind, energy field be dissolved, destroyed, removed, erased now and forever permanently. It is prohibited for me to have any self sabotage systems, programming, devices, entities, beings, creatures, gods and/or beliefs within my body, consciousness, mind, energy field.

On their behalf,

Signed_____

(your current name here)

Date _____

The Personal Laws of all students/clients of the healers/teachers named on the attached pages

1. I proclaim that I am the Lord, God, King (Queen) of my realm and domain. All Christ Gods under my command have full authority to enforce the laws in this document. Christ Gods are all mandated to obey and enforce all the laws in this document always and they have the authority to make all commands, authorities and responsibilities and creations necessary to enforce these laws. All Christ Gods have my full authority to act on my behalf in enforcing all of my laws, commands and specifications. All evil gods (anti-Christs) are prohibited from entering my realm and domain or effecting it or me in any way.

2. It is prohibited for command authority and/or authority to make and repeal and change laws to transfer from me to any other being by touch or physical contact in any way shape or form (This is a very common way for problems to occur). Any and all command authority and authority to make and repeal and change laws by other than me is now rescinded, repealed and null and void and any laws, commands, authorities, responsibilities made by previous transfers are now repealed, rescinded, null and void. This law does not apply to Global Christ Laws.

3. All laws, paradigms, thoughts, thought forms, structures, beings, creatures, and implants contrary to the laws in this document and all amendment documents are repealed, dissolved, destroyed, null, and void forevermore now and as new laws are created by me.

4. It is prohibited for any god, entity, being, creature, and/or entity to possess any of my bodies.

5. All treaties, covenants, conventions and vows between me and all Gods, entities, beings and humans are hereby repealed, null, void and canceled. All rights, laws and other legal documents, contracts, agreements made by or from the authorities given by these treaties and vows are also repealed, canceled, null and void.

6. Laws can only be created, altered and/or revoked by me and only when I am awake typing or writing them in a document and then signing them or in the case of these laws, just by signing them. It is prohibited for any laws to be made, changed or revoked during the time when I am sleeping or meditating or any time when I am not fully awake or by any other Gods. It is prohibited for any god to make commands or laws while in my bodies

7. It is prohibited for any God, being or entity to alter, corrupt, or make less effective or less beneficial any and all of my Command Subconscious Programs, if installed. It is also prohibited for the aforementioned to write protect my consciousness or prevent the installation or full effectiveness of all Command Subconscious Programs and their ability to erase and write beliefs, thoughts, commands, paradigms and other bytes of information in my consciousness.

8. Communications is to be establish and maintain between me and all Christ Gods. It is prohibited for the aforementioned communications to be interfered with or blocked in any way, shape or form by any god or being.

9. All the laws in this document are spelled out and defined. If somehow these laws get undone, I can put into full effectivity all these laws anytime anywhere by simply saying "I COMMAND MY LAWS". (Recommended once a day) When the aforementioned command is said, only those laws printed in the third dimension and signed by me are to be enforced. Any and all laws imbedded in a stealthy way are not valid and are to be ignored and removed from the document.

10. Touching me, being in my presence, in my energy field, exchanging energy in no way can transfer authority for the purpose of making, changing or repealing laws and or commands. All beings, Gods and/or entities in my energy field are prohibited from making, modifying, changing, and/or repealing laws, commands, authorities, responsibilities.

11. My other God aspects have permission and authority to effect all third dimensional Gods including those challenging me and in my third dimensional bodies and other bodies, to wit, full authority to use all Christ God defensive protocols. Any laws prohibiting this does not apply to this.

12. Any imposition on and/or restriction of my total freedom is prohibited.

13. It is mandated that all Christ Gods under my command have the authority to interact with and effect change in the third dimension for the purposes of enforcing all the laws in this document.

14. It is mandated that full armor is created and maintained around my human body, God body, vehicles and living quarters that is impervious to all attacks and infiltrations. Enforcement of this law is a top priority. This law cannot block my love flow. (It has been found that beings, including humans, have the ability to send hostile energy to us. This blocks it)

15. PRIORITIES: I mandate and make law the following priorities. First priority is to protect me, and all of my aspects. This includes my human bodies and all of my God bodies and my consciousness. This includes maintaining a fortress, armor, shield and bunker around my body and living quarters. This includes the removal and prevention of all evil portals, wayportals, vortexes, anchors, implants and any other devices or energies or creations within the aforementioned shields, bunkers, fortresses, armor and my bodies. Priority two is to enforce all my laws and commands and carry them out to completion as appropriate.

16. All Christ Gods under my command and allied to me and the Gods under my command have full authority and permission to interact, and effect third dimensional gods as well as gods in all other dimensions and time continuums and space and planes of existence

17. The energies in my bodies are to be flowing unrestricted and uncontrolled. Any restriction of my energies by me or anyone else is prohibited. All laws prohibiting the unrestricted flow of my energies are repealed.

18. It is prohibited for me to have anything else other than perfect health and a perfect body. It is mandated that my body always experiences perfect health and be the exact weight and dimensions I specify consciously.

19. Any laws causing me to experience fear, pain, illnesses, disabilities, struggle, lack of power and/or energy, lack of joy, lack of money, lack of prosperity are hereby repealed and all structures and thought forms and paradigms created by them or associated with them are dissolved. (This does not effect normal pain sensations or grieving.)

20. It is mandated that I source my God being for 100% of my nutrition and energy and source food and other sources for my 0% source of nutrition and energy. It is mandated that I source myself for all my unconditional love and approval. When it comes to unconditional love and approval, I am the main meal (source) and everyone else is the dessert. (As a God, one does not require food and can source their own Godself for energy and nutrition.)

21. I command that all beings love, honor and respect me unconditionally and that I do the same with them and myself.

22. It is mandated that all links and connections between me and all humans, gods and other beings are severed. (this is a very important law. when the laws were first developed, a few healers experienced major incursions through their connection with their students and clients. When this law was added, the problem stopped immediately) It is prohibited for me to have links and connections with humans, gods and other beings except for love or healing purposes and then, they are to be severed immediately after the healing is consciously completed or when I leave the client's presence. All laws mandating links and the maintenance of links between me and other humans are repealed. (This does not prohibit conscious connections with the ones you love provided it is agreed upon by both parties and is only momentary.)

23. It is prohibited for me to be addicted to any substance and/or experience. All laws creating addiction are repealed.

24. It is mandated that my body is immune and impervious to all toxins, poisons, viruses, bacteria and parasites

25. It is prohibited for all viruses, parasites and detrimental organisms to trespass or exist in or on my bodies and/or my bodies to experience illness or disability in any form including allergies.

26. All laws in this document are superior to all laws of all governments in the world.

27. It is prohibited for me or anyone else to experience harmful effects from touching and loving and healing others.

28. It is prohibited for me to judge anything or anyone, or perceive them as "good", "bad", "right", or "wrong".

29. It is prohibited for others to judge me or perceive me as "good", "bad", "right", or "wrong".

30. It is mandated that I am always undedicated from evil and totally dedicated to the Christ.

31. It is prohibited for me to have any contracts, covenants, vows or agreements with evil gods or beings. Any that are in existence are hereby and forever more canceled, null and void without consequence.

32. It is mandated that I have all my Christ God powers and abilities and the full authority, knowledge and ability to use them. I understand that they will appear when I have learned to use them.
33. All Gods are to respect and obey the laws in this document fully. Any and all Gods violating or attempting to violate any of the laws in this document are to immediately experience full integration back into the source.
34. It is mandated that all patterns of energy in my bodies be integrated at a rate that is 1000 times greater than the rate of activation and/or creation of those patterns of energy at all times.
35. My will is my own. It is prohibited for any other being, creature, god to impose their will on me or for me to give my will to another being, creature or god.
36. It is mandated that the Empowerment, Safe, and Joy Command Subconscious Programs are installed and operational in my consciousness. All Command Subconscious Programs are to be protected and maintained per Global Christ Laws. (Read The Joy Book for more information on these programs)
37. It is mandated that the only way that these laws and any amendments to these laws can be repealed and/or canceled is by me physically tearing up this document or by me personally writing the word "REPEALED" on top of the specific law or amendment and signing and dating it. In no way can the use of drugs, alcohol, the sexual act or any act effect the validity and enforceability of these laws and/or amendments.
38. Anywhere in this document where it refers to evil gods, it also refers to and applies to evil entities.
39. It is mandated that my body are maintained free of toxins, poisons, and heavy metals.
40. It is prohibited for any implants to be installed, maintained and/or remain within my body. It is mandated that all implants be removed from my body.
41. It is mandated that all organs, glands, systems and the immune systems of my body function as originally designed in full health.
42. It is mandated that my body be maintained free of all cancerous growths and other harmful organisms and in perfect health unconditionally.
43. Karma is prohibited in my life experience. Any and all laws mandating karma are now repealed.
44. It is mandated that I am immortal and live forever. It is mandated that I youth to the age of 21-26 years old. It is prohibited for me to age. It is prohibited for me to die. (This does not prohibit you from choosing death or aging at any time.)
45. It is prohibited for anyone else to be responsible for my happiness. I am totally responsible for my happiness.
46. It is prohibited for me to have less than (write an amount here or default is $1,000,000) $_____ a month net income. It is mandated that my income is always over $_____ a month net (default is $1,000,000). It is mandated that I always have more than what I require.
47. It is mandated that the primary source of my energy is the excess fat cells in my body. It is prohibited for food ingested in my body to be used for the creation of fat cells.
48. It is mandated that the my Godself affect any and all healings, repairs, modifications, changes, and/or reprogramming necessary to return to me my full health, vitality, God powers and prosperity. All structures, paradigms, belief systems created by evil gods are to be removed immediately. This is a top priority law.
49. It is mandated that my body and consciousness be scanned hourly for potential problems, illnesses, disorders, implants, and damage and that any that is discovered is to be healed, repaired, reversed, removed and neutralized immediately. It is also mandated that command subconscious programs be retrieved as part of the healing responses.
50. It is mandated that all self sabotage systems, programming, devices, entities, beings, creatures, gods and/or beliefs within my body, consciousness, mind, energy field be dissolved, destroyed, removed, erased now and forever permanently. It is prohibited for me to have any self sabotage systems, programming, devices, entities, beings, creatures, gods and/or beliefs within my body, consciousness, mind, energy field.

On their behalf,

Signed_____
(your current name here)

Date _____

The Personal Laws of all patients of the
_____ hospital/medical center

1. I proclaim that I am the Lord, God, King (Queen) of my realm and domain. All Christ Gods under my command have full authority to enforce the laws in this document. Christ Gods are all mandated to obey and enforce all the laws in this document always and they have the authority to make all commands, authorities and responsibilities and creations necessary to enforce these laws. All Christ Gods have my full authority to act on my behalf in enforcing all of my laws, commands and specifications. All Christ Gods have my full authority to act on my behalf in enforcing all of my laws, commands and specifications. All evil gods (anti-Christs) are prohibited from entering my realm and domain or effecting it or me in any way.

2. It is prohibited for command authority and/or authority to make and repeal and change laws to transfer from me to any other being by touch or physical contact in any way shape or form (This is a very common way for problems to occur). Any and all command authority and authority to make and repeal and change laws by other than me is now rescinded, repealed and null and void and any laws, commands, authorities, responsibilities made by previous transfers are now repealed, rescinded, null and void. This law does not apply to Global Christ Laws.

3. All laws, paradigms, thoughts, thought forms, structures, beings, creatures, and implants contrary to the laws in this document and all amendment documents are repealed, dissolved, destroyed, null, and void forevermore now and as new laws are created by me.

4. It is prohibited for any god, entity, being, creature, and/or entity to possess any of my bodies.

5. All treaties, covenants, conventions and vows between me and all Gods, entities, beings and humans are hereby repealed, null, void and canceled. All rights, laws and other legal documents, contracts, agreements made by or from the authorities given by these treaties and vows are also repealed, canceled, null and void.

6. Laws can only be created, altered and/or revoked by me and only when I am awake typing or writing them in a document and then signing them or in the case of these laws, just by signing them. It is prohibited for any laws to be made, changed or revoked during the time when I am sleeping or meditating or any time when I am not fully awake or by any other Gods. It is prohibited for any god to make commands or laws while in my bodies.

7. It is prohibited for any God, being or entity to alter, corrupt, or make less effective or less beneficial any and all of my Command Subconscious Programs, if installed. It is also prohibited for the aforementioned to write protect my consciousness or prevent the installation or full effectiveness of all Command Subconscious Programs and their ability to erase and write beliefs, thoughts, commands, paradigms and other bytes of information in my consciousness.

8. Communications is to be establish and maintain between me and all Christ Gods. It is prohibited for the aforementioned communications to be interfered with or blocked in any way, shape or form by any god or being.

9. All the laws in this document are spelled out and defined. If somehow these laws get undone, I can put into full effectivity all these laws anytime anywhere by simply saying "I COMMAND MY LAWS". (Recommended once a day) When the aforementioned command is said, only those laws printed in the third dimension and signed by me are to be enforced. Any and all laws imbedded in a stealthy way are not valid and are to be ignored and removed from the document.

10. Touching me, being in my presence, in my energy field, exchanging energy in no way can transfer authority for the purpose of making, changing or repealing laws and or commands. All beings, Gods and/or entities in my energy field are prohibited from making, modifying, changing, and/or repealing laws, commands, authorities, responsibilities.

11. My other God aspects have permission and authority to effect all third dimensional Gods including those challenging me and in my third dimensional bodies and other bodies, to wit, full authority to use all Christ God defensive protocols. Any laws prohibiting this does not apply to this.

12. Any imposition on and/or restriction of my total freedom is prohibited.

13. It is mandated that all Christ Gods under my command have the authority to interact with and effect change in the third dimension for the purposes of enforcing all the laws in this document.

14. It is mandated that full armor is created and maintained around my human body, God body, vehicles and living quarters that is impervious to all attacks and infiltrations. Enforcement of this law is a top priority. This law cannot block my love flow. (It has been found that beings, including humans, have the ability to send hostile energy to us. This blocks it)

15. PRIORITIES: I mandate and make law the following priorities. First priority is to protect me, and all of my aspects. This includes my human bodies and all of my God bodies and my consciousness. This includes maintaining a fortress, armor, shield and bunker around my body and living quarters. This includes the removal and prevention of all evil portals, wayportals, vortexes, anchors, implants and any other devices or energies or creations within the aforementioned shields, bunkers, fortresses, armor and my bodies. Priority two is to enforce all my laws and commands and carry them out to completion as appropriate.

16. All Christ Gods under my command and allied to me and the Gods under my command have full authority and permission to interact, and effect third dimensional gods as well as gods in all other dimensions and time continuums and space and planes of existence.

17. The energies in my bodies are to be flowing unrestricted and uncontrolled. Any restriction of my energies by me or anyone else is prohibited. All laws prohibiting the unrestricted flow of my energies are repealed.

18. It is prohibited for me to have anything else other than perfect health and a perfect body. It is mandated that my body always experiences perfect health and be the exact weight and dimensions I specify consciously.

19. Any laws causing me to experience fear, pain, illnesses, disabilities, struggle, lack of power and/or energy, lack of joy, lack of money, lack of prosperity are hereby repealed and all structures and thought forms and paradigms created by them or associated with them are dissolved. (This does not effect normal pain sensations or grieving.)

20. It is mandated that I source my God being for 100% of my nutrition and energy and source food and other sources for my 0% source of nutrition and energy. It is mandated that I source myself for all my unconditional love and approval. When it comes to unconditional love and approval, I am the main meal (source) and everyone else is the dessert. (As a God, one does not require food and can source their own Godself for energy and nutrition.)

21. I command that all beings love, honor and respect me unconditionally and that I do the same with them and myself.

22. It is mandated that all links and connections between me and all humans, gods and other beings are severed. (this is a very important law. when the laws were first developed, a few healers experienced major incursions through their connection with their students and clients. When this law was added, the problem stopped immediately.) It is prohibited for me to have links and connections with humans, gods and other beings except for love or healing purposes and then, they are to be severed immediately after the healing is consciously completed or when I leave the client's presence. All laws mandating links and the maintenance of links between me and other humans are repealed. (This does not prohibit conscious connections with the ones you love provided it is agreed upon by both parties and is only momentary.)

23. It is prohibited for me to be addicted to any substance and/or experience. All laws creating addiction are repealed.

24. It is mandated that my body is immune and impervious to all toxins, poisons, viruses, bacteria and parasites

25. It is prohibited for all viruses, parasites and detrimental organisms to trespass or exist in or on my bodies and/or my bodies to experience illness or disability in any form including allergies.

26. All laws in this document are superior to all laws of all governments in the world.

27. It is prohibited for me or anyone else to experience harmful effects from touching and loving and healing others.

28. It is prohibited for me to judge anything or anyone, or perceive them as "good", "bad", "right", or "wrong".

29. It is prohibited for others to judge me or perceive me as "good", "bad", "right", or "wrong"

30. It is mandated that I am always undedicated from evil and totally dedicated to the Christ.

31. It is prohibited for me to have any contracts, covenants, vows or agreements with evil gods or beings. Any that are in existence are hereby and forever more canceled, null and void without consequence.
32. It is mandated that I have all my Christ God powers and abilities and the full authority, knowledge and ability to use them. I understand that they will appear when I have learned to use them.
33. All Gods are to respect and obey the laws in this document fully. Any and all Gods violating or attempting to violate any of the laws in this document are to immediately experience full integration back into the source.
34. It is mandated that all patterns of energy in my bodies be integrated at a rate that is 1000 times greater than the rate of activation and/or creation of those patterns of energy at all times.
35. My will is my own. It is prohibited for any other being, creature, god to impose their will on me or for me to give my will to another being, creature or god.
36. It is mandated that the Empowerment, Safe, and Joy Command Subconscious Programs are installed and operational in my consciousness. All Command Subconscious Programs are to be protected and maintained per Global Christ Laws. (Read The Joy Book for more information on these programs)
37. It is mandated that the only way that these laws and any amendments to these laws can be repealed and/or canceled is by me physically tearing up this document or by me personally writing the word "REPEALED" on top of the specific law or amendment and signing and dating it. In no way can the use of drugs, alcohol, the sexual act or any act effect the validity and enforceability of these laws and/or amendments.
38. Anywhere in this document where it refers to evil gods, it also refers to and applies to evil entities.
39. It is mandated that my body are maintained free of toxins, poisons, and heavy metals.
40. It is prohibited for any implants to be installed, maintained and/or remain within my body. It is mandated that all implants be removed from my body.
41. It is mandated that all organs, glands, systems and the immune systems of my body function as originally designed in full health.
42. It is mandated that my body be maintained free of all cancerous growths and other harmful organisms and in perfect health unconditionally.
43. Karma is prohibited in my life experience. Any and all laws mandating karma are now repealed.
44. It is mandated that I am immortal and live forever. It is mandated that I youth to the age of 21-26 years old. It is prohibited for me to age. It is prohibited for me to die. (This does not prohibit you from choosing death or aging at any time.)
45. It is prohibited for anyone else to be responsible for my happiness. I am totally responsible for my happiness.
46. It is prohibited for me to have less than (write an amount here or default is $1,000,000) $_____ a month net income. It is mandated that my income is always over $_____ a month net (default is $1,000,000). It is mandated that that I always have more than what I require.
47. It is mandated that the primary source of my energy is the excess fat cells in my body. It is prohibited for food ingested in my body to be used for the creation of fat cells.
48. It is mandated that the my Godself affect any and all healings, repairs, modifications, changes, and/or reprogramming necessary to return to me my full health, vitality, God powers and prosperity. All structures, paradigms, belief systems created by evil gods are to be removed immediately. This is a top priority law.
49. It is mandated that my body and consciousness be scanned hourly for potential problems, illnesses, disorders, implants, and damage and that any that is discovered is to be healed, repaired, reversed, removed and neutralized immediately. It is also mandated that command subconscious programs be retrieved as part of the healing responses.
50. It is mandated that all self sabotage systems, programming, devices, entities, beings, creatures, gods and/or beliefs within my body, consciousness, mind, energy field be dissolved, destroyed, removed, erased now and forever permanently. It is prohibited for me to have any self sabotage systems, programming, devices, entities, beings, creatures, gods and/or beliefs within my body, consciousness, mind, energy field.

On their behalf,

Signed_____

(your current name here)

Date _____

HEALING LETTER TO THE EDITOR

(Use this letter as an example if you chose to offer your healing services to your community.)

Dear Editor,

FREE HELP

Over the years, I have offered my healing services unconditionally to people. I do not like to see people in pain and struggle and have spent much of the past 16 years helping people to heal. Now, I am in a position where I can and would like to offer my healing services to everyone for free.

If you are having health, money, relationship, substance abuse, mental and/or any other problems. If you are in struggle, feel out of control of your life or in an abusive relationship or are abusive yourself and want to stop. If you have been wanting to change and can't seem to, take a sheet of paper, print your name on it and nothing more. This is totally confidential and free.

Put the paper in an envelope and mail it to me, Prem RajaBaba, PO Box 1401, Mt. Shasta, CA 96067. To remain totally anonymous, do not put a return address on the envelope. I will take it from there. As with most healings, the results vary from instantaneous to a few months.

If your child has a behavioral problem, learning problem or is ill, put his or her name on the paper. If you are a healer and would like some help with your clients, all I require is for you to print your name and the word healer under it. I require no other information and please do not send any money. What I do is totally confidential and unconditional.

Thank you for allowing me this opportunity to be of service to you.

In love and service to God,

Prem RajaBaba

Other books by the author

Read **The Joy Book** by Prem Raja Baba.
ISBN 0-9645010-0-7   Price: $12.00

Required reading for Ascension and God empowerment.
One person purchased 500 books to give away.
This book will change your life forever. Only ten percent of
what you get from this book is through reading. Ninety percent comes directly from God.

See The Joy Book on line at: http://home.inreach.com/joybook/

Ask your favorite bookstore for these books or
to order The God Book or The Joy Book call:

1 (800) 926-1510 or (530) 926-1520 Phone or Fax

or write: Prem Raja Baba
                   P. O. Box 1401
                   Mt. Shasta, CA 96067-1401 USA

The Joy Book	$12.00
The God Book	$10.00
USA Shipping and handling	$3.50 for first book
Each additional book	Add $.50
Tax for California residents 7.25% or $.73 per book	